Homemade Christians II

Growing in the Dark

Written and Illustrated
by Nancy Marrocco

Novalis

Saint Mary's Press

Wood Lake Books

*"Be still
and know that I am God."*

Psalm 46:10

© Novalis, Saint Paul University, Ottawa, 1998.

Cover design, illustrations and page layout: Nancy Marrocco
Editors: Caryl Green and Michael Wilt

Novalis
49 Front St. East, Second Floor
Toronto, Ontario
M5E 1B3
1-800-387-7164 or (416) 363-3303

Wood Lake Books
9025 Jim Bailey Road
Kelowna, B.C.
V4V 1R2
1-800-663-2775

Canadian Cataloguing-in-Publication Data
Marrocco, Nancy
   Growing in the dark: homemade Christians II
ISBN 2-89088-856-8 (Novalis)
       1-55145-307-X (Wood Lake Books)
       0-88489-598-X (St. Mary's Press)

   1. Christian education of children. 2. Christian education—Home training. I. Title.
BV1475.2.M37 1998   248.8'45   C98-900013-3

Saint Mary's Press
702 Terrace Heights
Winona, MN 55987-1320 USA
1-800-533-8095

Printed in Canada

Dedicated
to a friend hidden
yet radiant

Table of Contents

I. I Shall Strengthen You

and give you

help

Isaiah 41:10c

This book is for you
who are mother or father,
one parent or two parents,
grandparent or godparent.

It's for all who want the children they love
to grow strong in the Christian faith.
It's for you who have tasted suffering.
It's for you who have glimpsed Light and want more of it.

This book
   is about
     a Light
       which shines
        so tenderly
         in the dark
          that the dark
        brings
        forth
        treasure.

Some think
that the child
whose faith will grow strongest
is the one whose parent's faith
is never shaken, never doubted, never questioned. Not true.

A child's faith can grow just as well
when the parent's way is dark, doubting or difficult.
What affects the child's growth
is the way the adult moves through
the doubt, darkness
and difficulty.

The more
we allow
God's Spirit
to lead us
through the dark,
learning the lessons
the Spirit teaches,
and receiving the treasures
God gives in the darkness,
the more our children will grow in faith.

This book is for those spiritually hungry enough
to reach for a God who can fulfill their deepest desires.

It's for anyone crazy enough
to consider that pain and dark
can give birth
to Light and joy.

It's for you
who so love your children
that you are brave enough
to grow in faith with them.

Save time . . .

Caring for a young child is hard work.
This book can lighten your burden by helping you see
how grace and Light can rush into
whatever you and your child are already doing.

Trust your own wisdom . . .

Practical activities and simple prayers are provided throughout.
Rather than telling you what your child should do at what age,
this book recognizes your little one as unique in all the world.
And you, as the expert on your own child,
the one who knows best what he or she is ready for at what age.

Relax . . .

You are attentive to your child's needs.
Be attentive to your own as you read this book.
Open it to whichever chapter offers you Light, help or hope as needed.
Whenever you find yourself led into prayer,
or struck by your own new insight or idea about raising your child in faith,
put the book down. Follow your heart. Trust your inner voice.
Move with the Spirit who is already moving within you and your child. Relax
and let God surprise you.

Here is a prayer you might keep in your office or kitchen.
Pray it as often as you like, maybe adding new words
of your own.

Spirit of Jesus, rise in me.
Awaken my depths.
Set me free.
Fill my heart with new confidence
and my soul with new hope.
May the children I love
grow strong in faith,
bathed in a Light
which is gentle,
tender
and bright.

II. You Are Holy

"The **Light** shines in the darkness, and the darkness has never mastered it."

John 1:5

You are
a temple of holiness.
Whatever your strengths or weaknesses might be, you are already radiant
with God's Light. God made you so.

"God's temple is holy, and you are that temple."

1 Corinthians 3:17

Take a candle and light it.
Carry it into a darkened room.
The room, perhaps, where Little Chris is now sleeping.
Find a pair of Chris's booties or shoes.
Cradle them gently
in your hand.

Know that you have been on a sacred journey.
A journey
which began so quietly
that you may not even have noticed.

It started when
you first desired
to love.

Read on by the light of your single candle shining in the dark.

Look at the candle you have lit.
It burns soundlessly.
It burns in the dark.
Your own deepest and holiest love for Chris
has been burning like that.
            Quietly.
                Soundlessly.
                    Somewhere
                        way down inside of you.
                        That love is burning now.

Try this simple prayer.
Still holding your child's shoes
and reading by candlelight,
slowly open your hand.
Become as still as you possibly can.

                    Ask God
            for one glimpse of who you are.
                    Wait expectantly,
            your open hand still bearing the shoes,
                    your mind and body
                as quiet as your burning candle.
            And allow God to show you the temple of holiness which you are.

When you are ready,
        place Chris's shoes
                at the foot of your lit candle,
                        as though you were placing them
                        at the feet of Jesus.
See these tiny shoes as a symbol
of the sacred journey.
Picture them
carrying
your child's feet
towards God.

                        Take off your own shoes.
                Place them near Chris's in the glow of the light.
        Ask God's blessing on Chris's travels and your own.
                Know that you do not travel alone.
                        The sacred journey is never made in isolation
                        but is guided, always,
                        by Someone who is sure-footed.
                Someone whose love burns with yours, way down inside.
                Blow out your candle, but don't worry.
                        You will find yourself
                        with Someone who knows a way through the dark.

14

III. Secrets

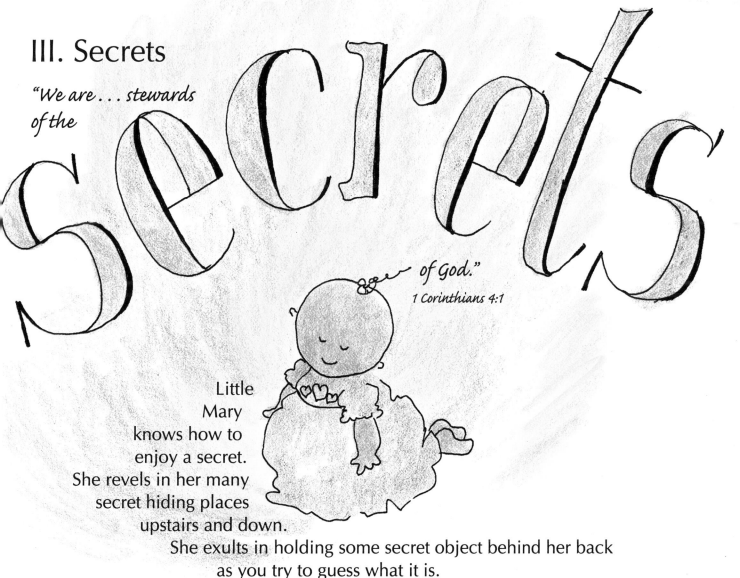

"We are . . . stewards of the

secrets

of God."
1 Corinthians 4:1

Little Mary knows how to enjoy a secret. She revels in her many secret hiding places upstairs and down. She exults in holding some secret object behind her back as you try to guess what it is.

One day you ask her a question.
She knows the answer.
But, instead of answering,
she grins and opens her eyes wide.
Beaming, she teases you,
        "Not telling! It's a secret!"

Another day, Mary comes to you
with a big ball of crumpled paper and tape.
She tells you that there is something special inside, a secret.
Joyous, she opens your hands
and entrusts her strange treasure into them.
She wants you to take care of it.

Mary has made you a steward of what is dear to her.
What is expected of the steward entrusted
        with a precious mystery?
        Mary wants you to respect her secret
        and take care of her treasure.
She may not say it in words,
but she asks that you reverence as sacred what she has given you.
And this young child expects something more:
that you wait until she chooses to open it and reveal its contents to you.

Notice that,
even without knowledge of what the secret is,
you are capable of doing as Mary asks.

Saint Paul says that God, too, has made you a steward of what is precious.
You, as servant of Christ, have been made a steward of the secrets of God.
God is trusting you to respect and care for this treasure in your heart.
You are asked to reverence this as sacred.

And you are asked something more:
to allow God's secrets to be revealed
when and how God chooses.
You did not demand that Mary reveal her secret to you
before you would agree to accept her precious treasure.
Instead, you received what she had given you,
honoured to be entrusted with something so dear to her.

God asks you to treat the most profound of mysteries
in this same way: honoured to be entrusted
with what is radically sacred,
with what is personally
God's.

Mary and Saint Paul agree on the job of a steward:
to be found trustworthy.

You are holy. You embody God's mysteries because God chose to give them to you.
You have the capacity to radiate God's Light to Mary,
even though you may not understand God's mysteries.

On some ordinary day
(not a special one like Christmas or a birthday),
wrap up a gift for Mary.
When you present her with this gift,
tell her it must stay secret
for a little while.
Assure her that it will be
a wonderful surprise
when the time comes
for her to open it.

Have her wait five or ten minutes before opening her gift,
or however long you think she can.

During the waiting time,
   encourage her to ask anything she wants about what's inside.
      Let her rattle it or shake it or turn it upside down.
         But don't give up the secret.

Did you know that, like you,
   Mary is a steward
      of God's mysteries?
      From the moment
         she was conceived,
         Mary has held
            the most sacred of God's secrets
            within her being.
         Mary was created
            in God's likeness,
            according to what
               God desired her to have
               and to hold.

   And from the very beginning,
   God was extravagant.

Raising a child in faith
is not about putting something into someone who doesn't have it yet.
It's about being opened up to what is already vibrant, living and holy
in both you and your child.

You are not expected to cause God to become present to Mary.
God is already with her.
You are expected to act as a trustworthy steward
of the mysteries God has entrusted to you. In doing that, you can
lead Mary to discover
what God has entrusted to her,
and to become
a trustworthy steward herself.

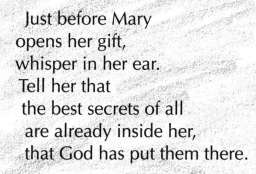

Just before Mary
opens her gift,
whisper in her ear.
Tell her that
the best secrets of all
are already inside her,
that God has put them there.

Expect no particular response.
Just tell her.

Then, as she opens her gift,
share her delight.
And say a prayer something like this . . .

God
of mystery and wisdom,
show me how to steward
all that You have placed in my heart,
and all that Mary gives into my hands.
Help me to trust
that You are revealing Your mysteries to us
as we are ready to receive them.

21

IV. You Are Not Lost

"If I fly with the wings of dawn
and alight beyond the sea,
Even there Your
hand will

guide

me..."

Psalm 139:9-10

Dominic loves to look up into the sky. He does not fear the secrets
inside himself, nor does he fear the secrets outside himself.
He is not afraid of immensity. He allows himself to taste mystery.
Not knowing the name of a single constellation, he delights in the beauty
and allure of each star. Dominic dwells daily in a universe infinitely bigger
than he is. Dominic dwells in awe before God.

You have seen much more of the universe than Dominic has.
Your sense of the sky might be different from his.
Standing before the endlessness and immensity of what is all around,
you may not be as calm as Dominic is.
There may even be days when you feel overwhelmed
by things you cannot comprehend.

On a starry night, look up into the sky with Dominic.
Tell him that God is something like the sky.
No one can see where the sky begins or ends.
And no one can see where God begins or ends.
Tell him there are lots of things about the sky that you don't know yet,
and lots of things about God that you don't know yet.
Tell Dominic that, if you and he could get to the end of the sky
or go to the farthest star, God could still find you there.
Because God gave the stars their places.
And God made the sky. And there is nowhere God cannot go.

Dominic
might like to hear
a story about the stars.
There is a particularly good one
embedded like a jewel
in the book
of the prophet Baruch (3:33-35).

As you are putting Dominic to bed
after seeing the stars,
tell him Baruch's story
in words
like these . . .

The Story of the Stars

God sends
out the stars.
God sends each one
to its own place.
And they all go on their way.

God calls the stars.
And, trembling,
they all come.

The
stars
shine
happily
in the places
God gives
them.

25

When God
calls the stars
they all answer,

"Here we are!"
"We are ready!"

They
shine brightly
for God
who made them.

There's a lot of theology here.
Baruch is saying that God is the powerfully creative source
of all things; that "trembling" is awe before God;
that there is an intimately personal relationship between God and creation;
that our highest joy is in responding to God, and in being all we can be with God.

One of the fascinating things about Dominic
is that his heart already "knows" such things.
So, don't worry about explaining any theology to him,
unless he asks and you feel you can.

After the story, ask Dominic which of the stars
on the last three pages he liked best. Print his name
on the star he chooses. Ask him to pick one for you.
Ask him why he picked that one.
Print your own name on the star he chose for you.
If he wants to dedicate other stars, help him do that.

Next time you're feeling lost,
banished to the sky's end,
or overwhelmed by things
bigger than you are,
say to God,
"Find me."

Give Dominic
some crayons and paper.
Ask him
to colour some stars
shining brightly
for God.
And, as he's colouring,
pray a prayer
like this:

You, O God,
know my appointed place.
You have given this place
to me and to no one else.
Call me. And I will answer, "Here I am."
But give me courage when I tremble, that I might say
"I am ready". Let us shine, Dominic and me,
let us shine and rejoice at our appointed places.

V. Becoming a Torch of Love

"Nothing can separate us from the **Love** of God..."

Romans 8:38

You know that the world can inflict hurt and loss. So,
you continually make choices in the interest of Clare's happiness and health:
bundling Little Clare into her snowsuit to protect her from winter's cold,
testing her bottle before giving it to her, so it isn't too hot, feeding her well
and ensuring she gets the necessary inoculations to ward off illness,
faithfully buckling her into her car seat.

You are a watchful and loving parent.

If you are like most parents,
you probably have a deep-down secret wish for Clare to be happy always.
For her to escape suffering. For her to never hurt anyone
or be hurt by anyone. For her life to be free of darkness.
For her faith to be so strong that she will never lose it.

> At Clare's baptism, you made a choice,
> the most extraordinary choice you could possibly make.
> On that day, a new white candle was dipped into the flame of Christ,
> a flame whose purpose is to burn with love always and in all places,
> even in deepest darkness. That small newly lit candle
> was then held out to you.
>
> Do you know why?
>
> It was not a sign that Clare should escape life's hurts.
> And it was not an inoculation against the darkness.
> As you received that candle for her, you made your choice.

And a proclamation was heard:
Clare was to become a torch of love, as Jesus Christ is a torch of love.
Clare was to enter the darkness, but never alone.
She would come burning with a Light which no darkness could overpower.
She would come accompanied and upheld, always, by God's Spirit, in God's love.

On the day you made that extraordinary choice,
Clare began her unique share in the transformation of this world's darkness.

Clare began a special relationship with Jesus Christ,
(that Someone who is sure-footed in the dark),
and with all those who seek His path.
She has her own unique purpose in the history of the world.
No one else can give the world what Clare can give it.
No one else will bring Light into the darkness in just the way that Clare will.

The next time you worry
about Clare's future,
or she gets sick or hurt,
or some force seems to threaten
her health or well-being,
take her baptismal gown
out of the closet.
Or find a photograph
from her baptismal day.
Or choose any other symbol
which speaks to you of her baptism
into the love and Light of Christ.
Place it near her bedside.

And, when your own anxiety is at its strongest,
light your little one's baptismal
candle again.

Then pray aloud Romans 8:38-39, with your child's name, like this:

"Neither death, nor life, nor angels,
nor principalities, nor present things, nor future things,
nor powers, nor height, nor depth,
nor any other creature will be able to separate Clare
from the love of God in Christ Jesus our Lord."

On Clare's baptismal anniversary, celebrate. Tell her where she was baptized and how people gathered around her in Church that day.
How water was poured over her and she was given a bath of Light.
Show her some photos. Show her the baptismal font at Church and tell her that's where her bath of Light took place. Teach her the date of her baptism.
Tell Clare about her godparents and other special people who came.
Invite them to a special meal. And pray a special grace, maybe like this:

Dear Jesus,
we thank you for Clare and for the Light
she brings. We thank you for this food.
Bless Clare so she can shine among us, in the dark and in the Light.
                                                        Amen.

And don't forget your own baptismal anniversary. Teach Clare you were bathed in the same Light she was. And celebrate.

VI. Even the Dark Is Graced

If you're still afraid
of darkness,
even after
baptism,
recall God's promise:

"I will give you

treasures

out of
the darkness
and riches that
have been hidden away."

Isaiah 45:3

What is darkness?

No matter where you live, the sun rises every day.
And every day the sun sets and darkness descends.

Is your Little Andy afraid of the dark? What scares him when the lights go out?
Is there any kind of darkness you fear? Why is it that you, a grown-up,
can still feel small, vulnerable and alone when darkness comes?

Wherever there is life, there is darkness. The dark of night.
The dark of death. The dark of doubt and confusion, of pain, of loss, of shame.

But this is not the full picture of darkness.
Before Andy was born, he lived in a world which knew no light.
He was warm, quiet and safe in the constant, sheltered darkness of the womb.
So were you, once. In the small and hidden world of the womb's total dark,
your heart started beating. And kept beating.
In the beginning, darkness was no impediment
to your growth, nor to Andy's.

"In the beginning,
God created the heavens and the earth.
The earth was a vast waste, darkness covered the deep,
and the spirit of God hovered over the surface
of the water."

Genesis 1:1-2

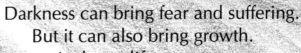

Darkness can bring fear and suffering.
But it can also bring growth.
And new life.
God's Spirit hovered over the waters
of the womb as Tiny Andy grew
in silent, wondrous dark.

Next time Andy (or you)
feels afraid of the dark,
show him this page.
And tell him about
the dark world of the womb
which held him snug and safe
when he was very very very tiny.
If there is a new baby
on the way,
tell Andy about how safe and comfortable
his new little brother or sister
is right now,
in the
womb's
total
darkness.

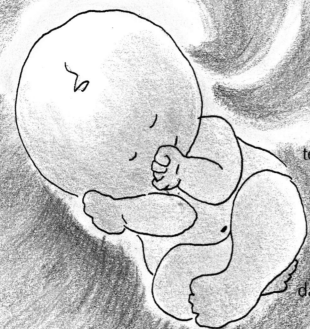

12

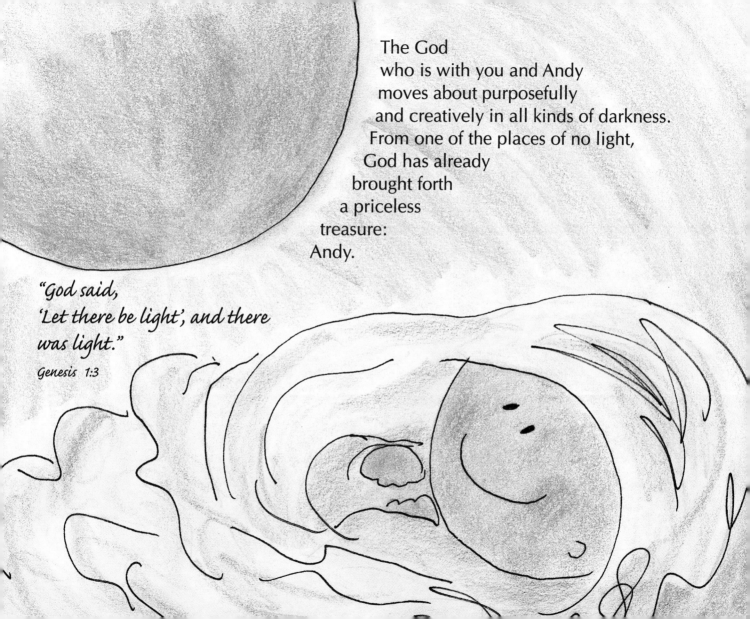

The God
who is with you and Andy
moves about purposefully
and creatively in all kinds of darkness.
From one of the places of no light,
God has already
brought forth
a priceless
treasure:
Andy.

"God said,
'Let there be light', and there
was light."

Genesis 1:3

The sacred journey is a journey like no other.

    Along its unpredictable path, darkness unexpectedly gives birth to Light.

       Joy is found growing where only pain had been.

Our God is an extraordinary and astonishing Lover, One who cannot
be driven away, turned back or confounded by any form of darkness.
One whose Light in Christ Jesus cannot be overcome.
One who will work a miracle in the dark or in the light.
As the psalmist exclaims,

"Even the darkness is not dark to you;
the night is as bright as the day,
for darkness is as light to you."

Psalm 139:12

For God knows the dark which oppresses and the dark which frees,
the dark which comforts and the dark which gives birth.

God knows the dark which frightens and the dark which condemns,
the dark which imprisons and the dark which isolates, breaks and destroys.
God knows the dark which calms and the dark which crushes,
the dark which teaches, nurtures and brings forth new growth.

All the ways of the dark are known to God.

And God knows
how to make the dark bend low
till it becomes
Tenderness in the night.

Next time
your child
is playing
in sandbox
or playpen,
having a bottle,
or taking
a nap,
pray aloud
the prayer
on the
next page.
Don't worry
whether
your little one
understands your
prayer,
or even is listening
to what you are saying.
Enough just to pray,
trusting that
God is hearing
every word you speak.

Enlighten
the eyes of our hearts
so that Andy
and I
may
know
what
is
the
hope
to
which Jesus has called us,
what are the riches of His glorious
inheritance among the saints,
and what is the immeasurable
greatness of His power
for us who believe . . .

(Adapted from Ephesians 1:18-19)

As you travel onward,
you will find that the sacred journey
winds its way through both dark places and light places.
In the dark places,
of course, you can't see what's happening.
So it can be hard to tell what God is offering you there.
And it usually hurts in such places. So it can be hard to stay in the dark
long enough for God to work a miracle in it.

Take a moment now to think back over your life and how you approach darkness.

Do you tend
to seek a quick escape
when dark times come?

Have you ever
judged the dark as waste
before giving God a chance
to make it bear fruit?

In the midst of suffering, most of us find it hard to trust that real Light
can come into real dark. Escape appears easier.
Next time you find yourself veering off the path
when it's heading into a dark stretch, or find yourself resisting whatever is called for
by the sacred journey, tell your child "The Story of the Unwanted Gift."

The Story
of the Unwanted Gift

One day,
a friend brought a surprise.
Some gifts for Little Andy and Little Roberto.
Roberto was very happy with his gift.

But Andy was very unhappy with his.
All Andy got were two small square things
in a plain wrapper.

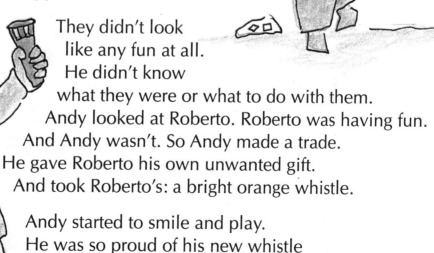

They didn't look
  like any fun at all.
  He didn't know
what they were or what to do with them.
  Andy looked at Roberto. Roberto was having fun.
  And Andy wasn't. So Andy made a trade.
He gave Roberto his own unwanted gift.
  And took Roberto's: a bright orange whistle.

Andy started to smile and play.
He was so proud of his new whistle
 that he forgot all about
        the two small square things in their plain wrapper.

But then Andy noticed that Roberto was having fun
with those square things. Roberto had found something amazing
about the gift which was first given to Andy.
Those two little square things were like magic.
They could stick to all kinds of other things.
They could hang upside-down, all by themselves.
They could even pull Roberto's toy truck all around the room.
Those two square things had a power all their own.

Roberto had discovered that the two small squares were magnets.

Andy got tired of blowing his whistle
long before Roberto got tired of the magnets.
When Andy saw all the fun Roberto
was having with the magnets,
he wanted them back.
But Roberto
wouldn't give them back.

Andy lost his gift
because he gave it away so fast.
He gave it away
before he knew
what he had.

Could God be offering you something good right now, in the dark, something you really need? Pause for a moment to ponder this possibility.

Sometimes, gifts which come from the dark are the finest gifts of all, treasures not found anywhere else.

Whenever Andy immediately pushes away something you give him (a new food, a new drink, a new shirt), push it back gently, but firmly.

Insist he explore it, taste it or touch it at least until he knows what he's pushing away.

Next time you're shopping, buy a fridge magnet.

Keep it for notes about trusting God in the dark. Make up your own, or borrow from Psalms 18, 34 or 56, from Jeremiah 17:7-8 or John 4:7-14 or any other passage you like.

If you think it's appropriate, tell Andy what some of your notes are about. Get a fridge magnet for him.

When he's old enough to colour, let him colour a picture about God helping him in the dark.

VII. Breaking Free of Perfectionism

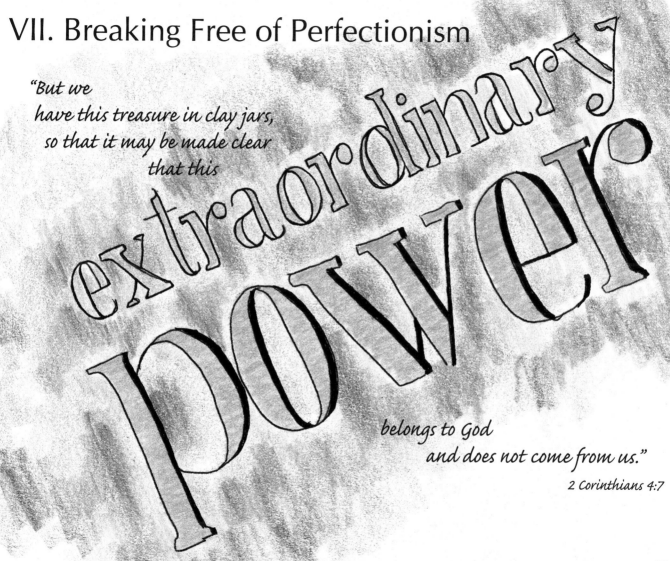

"But we have this treasure in clay jars, so that it may be made clear that this extraordinary power belongs to God and does not come from us."

2 Corinthians 4:7

One day, Little Andrea dumped all the tea
out of the tea bags. She thought she was helping.
But you scolded her a little more harshly than she deserved.
Later, she cried and cried for you to come and play with her. But you didn't.

Andrea discovered a ladybug.
She was so excited, so proud. She talked
your ear off about that ladybug.
But you really paid very little attention
as she spoke.

Andrea fell
and scraped
her knee — again.
But you just didn't
feel like kissing it
and making it better.
So you didn't.

You vaguely recall hearing that you are a temple of the
Holy Spirit, a vessel bearing God's holiness in this world.
You have even heard that, dwelling inside of you,
is the radiant, unimaginable Light of Christ.
But sometimes you don't feel like a dwelling place for God.
You are alarmed to find yourself unmoved
by the tears pouring down Andrea's cheeks.

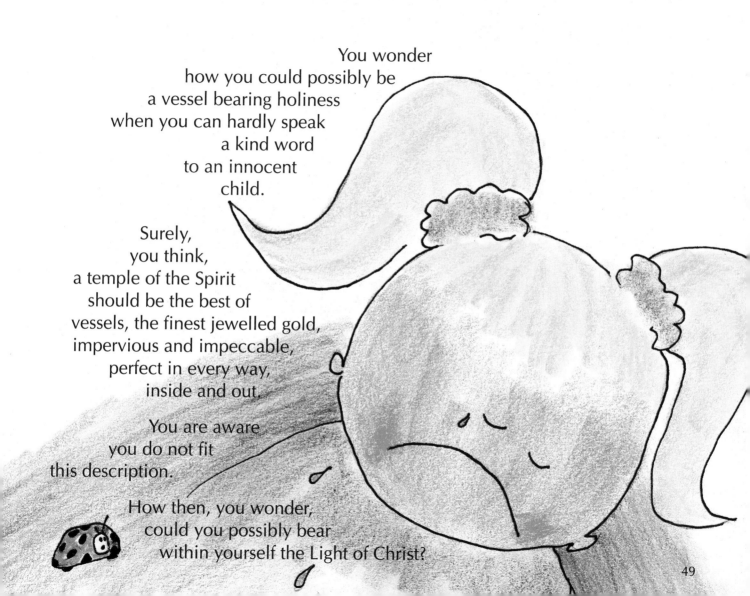

You wonder
how you could possibly be
a vessel bearing holiness
when you can hardly speak
a kind word
to an innocent
child.

Surely,
you think,
a temple of the Spirit
should be the best of
vessels, the finest jewelled gold,
impervious and impeccable,
perfect in every way,
inside and out.

You are aware
you do not fit
this description.

How then, you wonder,
could you possibly bear
within yourself the Light of Christ?

You recall the shining day your child
was baptized. "Yes," you
declared for all the Church
to hear, "Yes, I will bear
the Light of Christ
for Andrea."
Inwardly you dreamed
of being the best of
Christian parents,
a flawless gold cup
tipped to Andrea's lips
that she might drink
deeply of God.
But we are clay jars.
Faulted and imperfect.
Bumpy.
Breakable.
And not always
shining.

But God wanted a clay jar for Andrea.
God did not choose a golden goblet for her.
God chose you, with all your imperfection and fragility.
God chose you to be the first one to bear the Light of Christ for Andrea.

God loves to pour Light into clay jars. This is God's specialty.
You are God's delight, a clay jar holding an extraordinary power
that belongs to God and comes from God.

This power is God's treasure. It cannot be destroyed by your
failures or limitations. Neither God nor Andrea expect you to be perfect.
In recognizing the truth, you begin
to break free, free to belong to God.
And you begin to teach Andrea
that she, too, bears the unimaginable
Light of Christ
—without being perfect.
That she, too, is a clay jar.
And that God has a fondness
for clay jars.

On Sundays, Andrea is drawn to the shiny gold
candle-holders and other gold touches in the church.
One day she asks, "Why is there so much gold in church?"

And you can tell her that God made us to shine like gold.
But that, for us to shine, we must start out like clay.

After church, give Andrea
a lump of playdough or clay.
If Joey is around,
let him join in too.
Take some for yourself.
Together bend
and stretch and shape
and sculpt your lumps,
any which way
you want to.
Look at Andrea and
Joey. See that they are
made in the image
and likeness of God.

Quietly ponder God's choice to start us out like clay.

When you feel
fragile, flawed
or broken, hold
some clay in your hand
and pray for your little one:

My child,
God looks at you and sees someone more precious
than gold. God knows we are made of clay.
Yet God sees us already shining. God of tender love,
teach us to cherish the clay which we are.

VIII. Letting Go of Doubt

"*Happy* are they
who find faith
without seeing me."

John 20:29b

Do you believe without seeing?
Or do you insist on seeing first?

When Little Stephen has learned
to count to three, invite him to play
a game called "Seeing in the Dark."
Have Stephen close his eyes
and hold out his hands.
Tell him to keep his eyes closed
till you say he can open them.

Then, in his hands, place three small stones.

Ask Stephen to count the stones without opening his eyes.
Just by feeling them with his hands.

Now, let Stephen open his eyes.
Ask him how he was able
to count the stones
without being able to see them.
If he can't tell you, explain that,
even though his eyes
couldn't see the stones,
his hands could,
by feeling them.

Hands have
their own
special way
of "seeing".

Tell Stephen that he can see
lots of things with his eyes.
And that he can see lots of things with his hands.

But best of all is . . .

. . . what he can see with his heart.

                    Tell Stephen
               that hearts can see God
                 even though eyes can't.
                    Because that's how God made us.

Now, this may be another of those things
that Stephen already knows, deep down.
But, tell him anyway.
Putting such things into words once in a while
can help Stephen learn to articulate and understand in his head
those things his heart has already known.

As Stephen grows up, he will begin to discover
that he lives in a culture which places a greater value
on what is seen than on what is unseen.
                    A culture which looks more
                       to scientific proof
                    than to inner trust.

               Teach Stephen to value the unseen.

"...for what can be seen is temporary, but what cannot be seen is eternal."

2 Corinthians 4:18b

Ask Stephen to close his eyes again.
Tell him to stretch out his hands
as wide as he possibly can.
In one hand, place a treat.
In the other, a kiss.
Ask him to tell you
—with his eyes still closed—
what you gave him.

Ask Stephen how he knows.
Then let him open his eyes and have his treat.
As he munches,
read the story
of Doubting Thomas
(to Stephen, or just to yourself).
It's John 20:24-31.

After you've read the story,
ponder this: the disciples told Thomas
that Jesus was risen from death,
but Thomas refused to believe
until he could see the wounds in Jesus' hands and feet and side.

Eight whole days went by
as Thomas continued to doubt.
Then Jesus came.
Jesus showed Thomas the holes.
And then He told Thomas something that probably
surprised Thomas, and may surprise us.
Jesus told his friend, "Happy are they who find faith without seeing me."

Why should believing without seeing
make a person happy?

Because the heart
can experience far more
than the eyes can see.
The heart can begin
to rejoice
while the eyes
are still blind,
long before
the eyes can see
anything at all.
Faith is a way
of seeing
in the dark.

Thomas could not believe until he saw with his eyes. He was locked inside his own blindness, grief and darkness. He missed out on something good by insisting on seeing first. If Thomas could have believed before seeing, he would not have had to live through eight days of doubt and darkness.

He could have met the Risen Jesus in his heart right then and there. Thomas could have had eight days of joy.

As we grow older, we learn to doubt.

Happy is Little Stephen. He is still young enough to believe in Jesus without depending on his eyes to see Him.

60

Take three small objects — buttons perhaps, or stones, each of a different size. When you have a moment to yourself, hold the smallest of the three in your hand. Sit down and close your eyes.

Let this small object represent one area of doubt in your life. Explore this object, just by feel. As you do, think about how this doubt affects your life. Then ask God to help you see with the eyes of faith. Now take the middle-sized object and do the same with an area of doubt which is a little larger than the first. Then take the largest object and, with courage, ask God to show you that area of doubt in your life which is most depriving you of happiness and freedom.

Happy are you if you believe that God, unseen, will answer your prayers.
Happy are you if you believe that God already dwells in Stephen's heart, and Stephen in God's.
Happy are you. Even though your eyes cannot see.

On another day, get some seeds.
Invite Stephen to help you plant them in a corner of the yard.
If he's too young for that, just let him watch you.
If it's wintertime, plant your seeds indoors in small pots.

Show Stephen how the seeds get buried deep down in the soil.
Let him push one or two seeds down deep so he can feel
how they get all covered up, and seem to have disappeared.

If he asks some "Why?" questions, exult in them.
Such questions are the life of the soul. Just answer as well as you can.

Visit this small garden with Stephen each day,
especially in the first few days of germination
when there is no evidence of growth at all.
Tell him what's happening beneath the surface:
the seeds are sprouting in secret darkness,
growing, though we cannot see them.

*"This is what
the kingdom of God is like.
A man scatters seed on the land.
Night and day, while he sleeps, when he is awake,
the seed is sprouting and growing; how, he does not know."*

Mark 4:26-27

Another day,
as you look down at the soil together,
try this simple prayer with Stephen . . .

Close your eyes and stretch out your hands
as wide open as you can. Ask Stephen to do the same.
Pray aloud something like this,
"God, put what we need into our hands."

Since young children naturally imitate what grown-ups do,
Stephen might spontaneously echo your prayer.
If he does, be glad. If he doesn't, don't worry.
Thank God for taking care of things in secret,
for giving you and Stephen gifts you can see
and gifts you can't see.

Open your eyes and let Stephen open his.
If the moment seems right for it, ask Stephen to thank God
for something he can see with his eyes.
And then for something he can see with only his heart.

As opportunities present themselves,
teach Stephen to exult in God's love:
both when God's creative work bursts into view,
and when it lies completely hidden from sight.

As Stephen grows, remember that faith is a marvelously, mysteriously hidden sort of thing.

Stephen weighed six pounds five ounces at birth. He had two teeth at seven months. He spoke eight words at ten months. He wore size 3X at twenty-four months. Stephen's physical growth can be measured in all these ways.

But no one can measure Stephen's growth in faith. There are no standardized guidelines about what quantity of faith a young child should have by what age, or how that should look.

There is no size 3X or 10X when it comes to faith. It's much too hidden and personalized for that.

So, when it comes to measuring the growth of Stephen's faith,
you will find yourself in the dark.
The best way to resolve this problem is to not try.
Because, if you persist in trying to measure your child's faith growth,
you will succeed only in trying to measure your own success or failure as a parent.
And then your focus will be much more on what you can do
than on what God can do.
This is dangerous.

What happens is that, when we find our measurements yielding no results
(as they surely will, because faith cannot be measured),
we will probably conclude that we have failed as Christian parents.
Preoccupation with our own failure feelings will be of no help to Stephen.
This preoccupation breeds doubt and blindness.

What Stephen needs is for you to keep your focus on God,
relying on God's mysterious and trustworthy ways of teaching,
God's power to bring forth new growth in the dark,
God's unfathomable, abiding love.

Helping a young child to grow in faith is a lot like planting seeds.
It would do no good to dig up seeds each day
to see how many had sprouted or how much they had grown.
Better just to water them regularly and wait in hope.

As you go along,
pray to be freed
of anything
which takes
your focus
away
from
God's love.

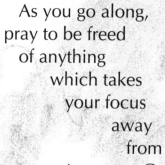

Then,
just keep doing
what you can.
And leave
the rest
to God
and
Stephen.

After all,
it's not
that God has a small share
in your job of bringing Stephen to faith.
It's that you have a small share
in God's bringing Stephen to faith.

Some night,
when it's really good and dark,
and Stephen is sleeping,
go to his room.

Know that Stephen's faith
is growing in secret,
like the seed
buried deep
in the
ground.

Pray aloud over Stephen
as he sleeps:

"Though the fig tree does not blossom,
and no fruit is on the vines . . .
yet I will rejoice in the Lord;
I will exult in the God
of my salvation.
God, the Lord, is my strength . . ."

Habakkuk 3:17ff

Leave your Bible
in Stephen's room
for a few days, open
to the fig tree passage.

Another night,
try a prayer
like Habakkuk's:

*"Though
Stephen's faith
is growing in secret
where I cannot see it,
though its blossoms, when they come,
may be invisible to my eyes,
and its fruits be slow
to appear on the vines,
yet I will exult
in the God of my salvation"*

Stay still. Look out
Stephen's window
into the dark night.
Listen for God's voice.

IX. Daring to Hope

Remember Doubting Thomas? Perhaps you are willing to admit that Thomas would have been better off to believe before seeing. But, you can't help wondering, what if Jesus had come to Thomas not after eight days, but after eight months or even after eight years? How could Thomas have managed to wait and believe that long before seeing with his eyes?

Sometimes the wait for God feels long, unbearably long.
Sometimes God seems incredibly slow to respond.
And yet,

"*The Lord takes pleasure . . . in those who* Hope *in his steadfast love*"

Psalm 147:11

Twins sisters Ruth and Loretta are wild with excitement. Their birthday is coming and they've been promised a party. They jump up and down, crying out "Oh when? When? When will it be our birthday???".

This is the zeal of little ones who have allowed their whole being to be filled with intensely expectant, joy-filled longing. So focussed are the twins on the single cherished hope of their birthday coming, that they can think of nothing else.

Loretta and Ruth are waiting. With joyful expectancy. With confident hope. How do you wait for the good things promised to you in Christ Jesus?

You've learned that God can make the dark fertile.
But you also know that most of the seeds
you and God plant in the dark won't sprout overnight.
How, then, do you wait
for the sprouting, budding and blossoming?

Ruth and Loretta wait
with whole-souled expectant joy-tinged longing.

Is there any
of that glorious childlike quality
left in a grown-up
like you?

Do you allow yourself
to truly long
for what God
has promised?

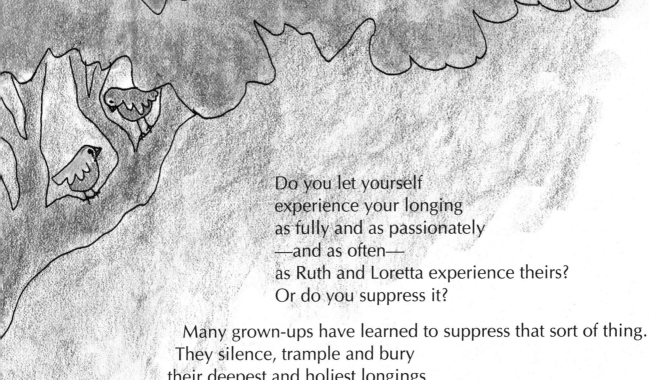

Do you let yourself
experience your longing
as fully and as passionately
—and as often—
as Ruth and Loretta experience theirs?
Or do you suppress it?

Many grown-ups have learned to suppress that sort of thing.
They silence, trample and bury
their deepest and holiest longings
out of fear that nothing good will really come.

What about you?
Have you found it safer to not hope?
The little ones are waiting in hope.

Are you?

Because they are still young, the twins' joy-filled longing is still healthy. As they grow, they will have to learn to manage their excitement so that they can get on with other things as they wait.

But you, already grown-up, may have gone too far the other way: afraid of your own holiest longings because you've been wounded by life's hurts, disappointments and failings. You, too fearful to hope, and the children too hope-filled to sit still. Somewhere in between lies a balance.

Ruth and Loretta dare to hope. Let their capacity for hope rekindle your own.

In Psalm 147, we learn that God delights not in the type of human sturdiness
that causes us to plod on in despair.
God delights in "those who hope in his steadfast love."
God delights in Ruth and Loretta.
Neither has any power to cause their birthday party to come any sooner than it will.
Neither can make the birthday cake rise faster in the oven.

But, in their inborn unsullied wisdom,
they have already begun to rejoice, in the very midst of their waiting.
These little ones live not only the joy of their birthday when it does come,
but all the hope-and-joy-filled anticipation leading up to it as well.

God delights
in the child and in the childlike
because happiness is found
in the hoping
as well as in the having.

When the birthday cake
is finally baked and frosted
and all is ready, light the candles.
And light an extra one, right in the middle of the cake.
Light it as a symbol of your own willingness
to let God fill you to the brim with hope.

As Ruth and Loretta
make their wishes,
    allow your own
    deepest hope
    to rise.

75

Remember, Christian hope
is not an emotion.
It's the willingness
to place your trust
not in your strength
but in God's.

When the choice
to hope in God is made,
new emotion comes along with it
—peace, solace, encouragement,
confidence, well-being, joy.
Even before you can see
what God is doing.
Even while the seed lies buried.
Choose hope.
And keep choosing it.
Until you come to expect
God's help.
Trust that God is already
in the process of answering all the prayers you've ever prayed,
in the Light and in the dark.
Before going to the next page, stop to imagine
what life might be like if you trusted as much as that.

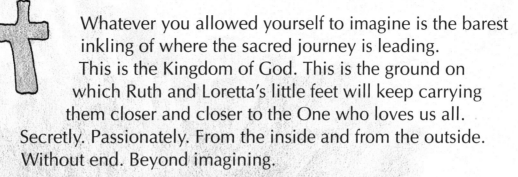

Whatever you allowed yourself to imagine is the barest
inkling of where the sacred journey is leading.
This is the Kingdom of God. This is the ground on
which Ruth and Loretta's little feet will keep carrying
them closer and closer to the One who loves us all.
Secretly. Passionately. From the inside and from the outside.
Without end. Beyond imagining.

In the evening after the birthday party,
pray this prayer
for your little ones:

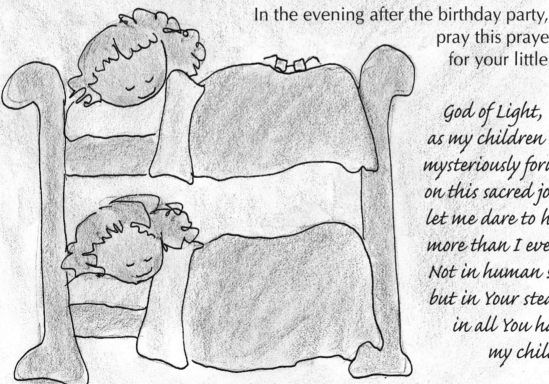

God of Light,
as my children move
mysteriously forward with You
on this sacred journey,
let me dare to hope a little
more than I ever have before.
Not in human sturdiness
but in Your steadfast love,
in all You have promised
my children and me.

Finish this book
  knowing that the God
    who sings us a lovesong, whether
      we are standing in the Light or in the dark,
    will sing to you and your children
      the whole of your journey.

        God's song
          sounds
            like this . . .

"Come, then, my beloved, my lovely one, come.
For see, winter is past,
   the rains are over and gone.

Flowers are appearing on the earth.
The season of glad songs has come,
the cooing of the turtledove is heard in our land.

The fig tree is forming its first figs,
   and the blossoming vines
                  give out
                        their fragrance.
                  Come then,
                        my beloved,
                           my lovely one,
                              come."

Song of Songs 2:10-13

The seed is planted.
And you do the watering.
But, like Saint Paul
says,

"God gives the growth."

1 Corinthians 3:6